# PIRATES

Philip Steele

Kingfisher
NEW YORK

KINGFISHER
Larousse Kingfisher Chambers Inc.
95 Madison Avenue
New York, New York 10016

First edition 1997
10 9 8 7 6 5 4 3 2

Copyright © Larousse plc 1997

LIBRARY OF CONGRESS CATALOGING-
IN-PUBLICATION DATA
Steele, Philip,
    Pirates / Philip Steele.—1st American ed.
        p. cm.
    Includes index.
    Summary: Discusses when and where
pirates typically lived and what their
activities were.
1. Pirates—Juvenile literature.
[1. Pirates.]  1. Title. G535.S746
1997  910.4'5—dc20  96-34542
CIP AC

ISBN 0-7534-5052-6

Author: Philip Steele
Consultant: David Cordingly
Editor: Molly Perham
Design: Ben White
Cover design: Robert Perry
Art editors: Christina Fraser
  and Sue Aldworth
Picture research: Image Select
Printed in Italy

# CONTENTS

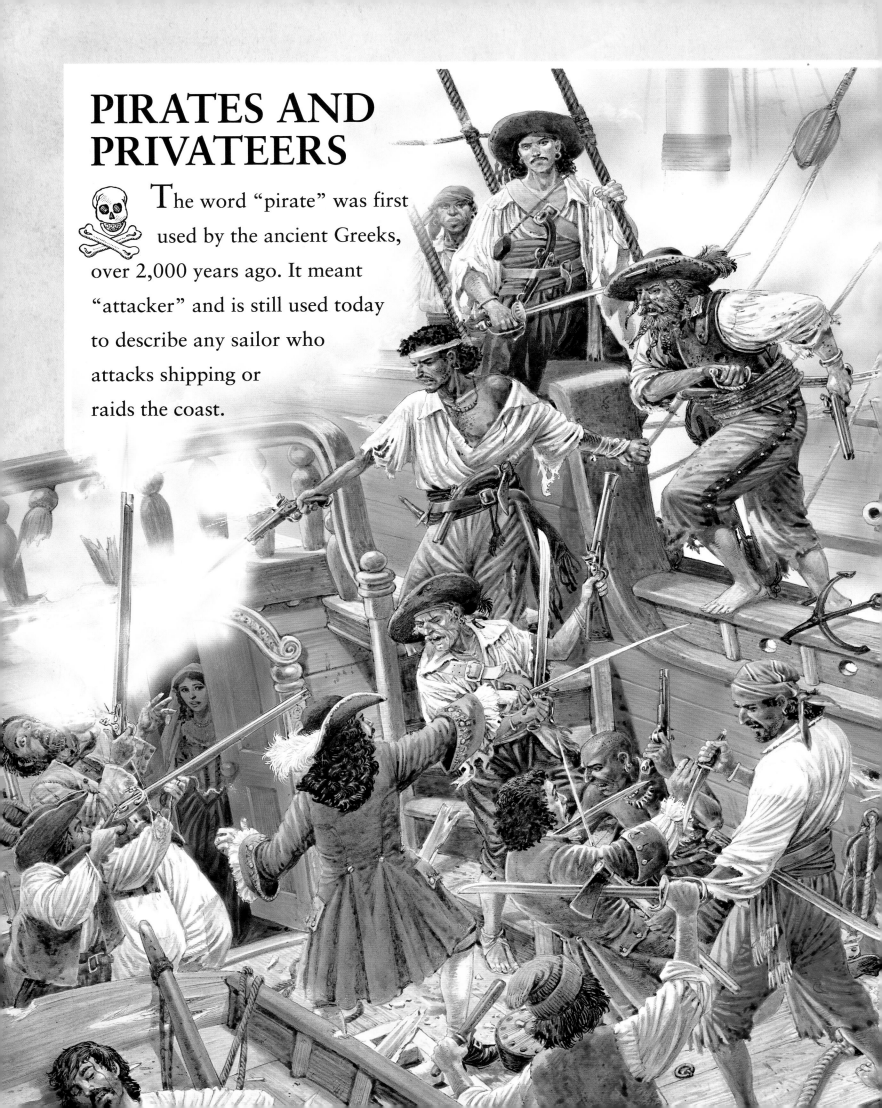

# PIRATES AND PRIVATEERS

The word "pirate" was first used by the ancient Greeks, over 2,000 years ago. It meant "attacker" and is still used today to describe any sailor who attacks shipping or raids the coast.

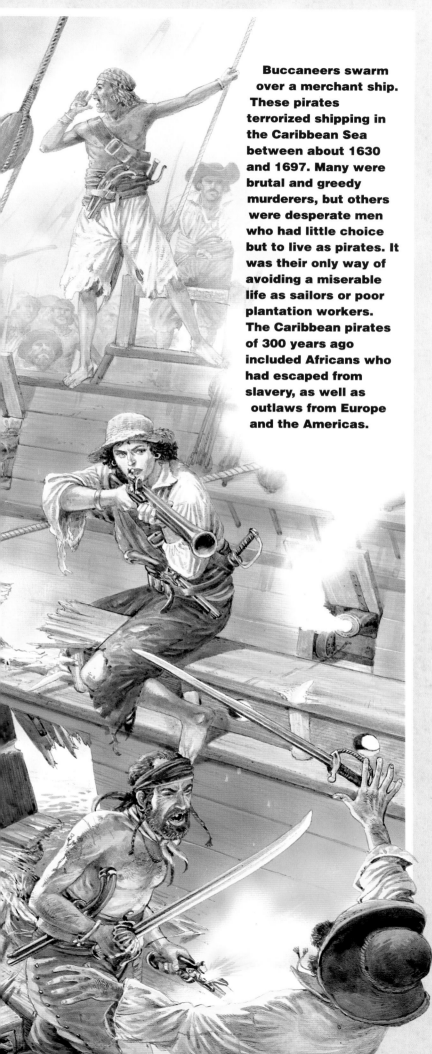

Buccaneers swarm over a merchant ship. These pirates terrorized shipping in the Caribbean Sea between about 1630 and 1697. Many were brutal and greedy murderers, but others were desperate men who had little choice but to live as pirates. It was their only way of avoiding a miserable life as sailors or poor plantation workers. The Caribbean pirates of 300 years ago included Africans who had escaped from slavery, as well as outlaws from Europe and the Americas.

▲ This old chart shows Francis Drake's attack on Cartagena in 1586. Four hundred years ago Cartagena, in Colombia, was a port for the Spanish treasure fleet.

In 1581, Queen Elizabeth I made Francis Drake a knight. To the English, Drake was a national hero. To the Spanish, he was nothing but a common pirate.

Many other words have been used to describe pirates. Corsairs, buccaneers, rovers, filibusters, and freebooters ... all were pirates of one kind or another. Sometimes governments licensed private shipowners to attack the merchant vessels of another country with whom they were at war. These lawful pirates were called "privateers," and they shared the profits with the government. Many respectable seafarers like Francis Drake turned pirate from time to time. And many governments secretly backed pirate expeditions—provided the pirates shared the booty with them!

# Clues to the past

How do we find out the truth about piracy? Many stories about pirate captains and buried treasure are little more than tall tales. How can we prove when and where a ship was sunk? On land, archaeologists can dig up remains from the past and find out how old they are. Marine archaeology is harder. Shipwrecks may be buried or scattered. Divers may have to work in dangerous conditions in deep water.

How do archaeologists know which ship they have found? At this wreck, divers discovered the ship's bell, engraved with the words THE WHYDAH GALLY 1716.

### Marine archaeology
The English ship *Whydah* traded in slaves, sugar, indigo dye, and ivory. In February 1717, the ship was captured by the pirate Sam Bellamy. It went down during a storm off Cape Cod in Massachusetts, in April 1717. It sank in shallow water, but lay hidden in deep sand for 266 years.

## Piratical documents

Some buccaneers of the 1600s and 1700s, such as Basil Ringrose and William Dampier, left behind logbooks, charts, and stories of their travels. The most famous account was *Bucaniers of America* by the French buccaneer Alexandre Exquemelin, which was first published in Amsterdam in 1678.

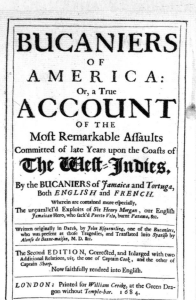

BUCANIERS
OF
AMERICA:
Or, a True
ACCOUNT
OF THE
Moſt Remarkable Aſſaults
Committed of late Years upon the Coaſts of
**The Weſt-Indies,**
By the BUCANIERS of *Jamaica* and *Tortuga,*
Both *ENGLISH* and *FRENCH.*

Wherein are contained more eſpecially,
The unparallel'd Exploits of *Sir Henry Morgan,* our Engliſh
*Jamaican* Hero, who ſack'd *Puerto Velo,* burnt *Panama,* &c.

Written originally in *Dutch,* by *John Eſquemeling,* one of the *Bucaniers,*
who was preſent at thoſe Tragedies; and Tranſlated into *Spaniſh* by
*Alonſo de Bonne-maiſon,* M.D. &c.

The Second EDITION, Corrected, and Inlarged with two
Additional Relations, viz, the one of *Captain Cook,* and the other of
*Captain Sharp.*
Now faithfully rendred into Engliſh.

*LONDON:* Printed for *William Crooke,* at the Green Dra-
gon without *Temple-bar.* 1684.

◄ **The wreck of the *Whydah* was eventually discovered in 1983 by an American diver named Barry Clifford. Instead of its normal cargo, it contained Sam Bellamy's pirate treasure of gold and silver coins, gold bars, parts of swords, muskets and pistols, cannons and grenades, and a leather pouch and shoe.**

Another way we can find out about the past is by reading old inscriptions, gravestones, and books. But we cannot believe every word we read. Some writers exaggerated the facts or claimed that their enemies were pirates when they weren't. There are other references to piracy in old law books and reports of trials and executions. In the 1600s and early 1700s, the lands of North America and the Caribbean were colonies, ruled by European nations. Colonial governors sent in reports about piracy, and these can still be read today.

## Found on land

Archaeology on dry land tells us about the daily life of pirates ashore. Many had bases in ports or on remote islands around the world. Rum bottles, tankards, candlesticks, spoons, and brass buckles were discovered at Port Royal, the Jamaican pirate base destroyed by an earthquake in 1692.

▲ In Roman times, antipiracy patrols used galleys—long ships with banks of oars and single sails. Galleys had a ram at the front to sink enemy vessels. The galleys were full of Roman troops, but pirates often got the better of them.

◄ Cilician pirates were feared in the Mediterranean for their cruelty. They had a barbarous custom of tying prisoners back to back and throwing them into the sea.

# TERROR IN EUROPE

The ancient seafaring peoples of the Mediterranean, such as the Phoenicians, Cretans, and Greeks, were great traders—and pirates, too. Greek towns were hemmed in by mountains or coasts, so many Greeks sailed off to find new lands for themselves in Italy, France, and Spain. They often attacked shipping and coastal towns. Over 2,500 years ago the Lipari Islands became a full-time base for Greek pirates.

▼ By A.D. 250, the Roman Empire included most of Europe and parts of Asia and Africa. The Roman navy ruled the waves.

But within 150 years its power had weakened. As Roman troops pulled out of Britain, Saxon and Irish pirates moved in.

## Caesar captured

In 78 B.C. a young Roman called Julius Caesar was serving in a naval action against pirates from Cilicia, in what is now Turkey. The pirates captured the young nobleman and held him hostage on the island of Pharmacusa until the Romans paid them a big ransom. The Cilician pirates rampaged across the Mediterranean for another 11 years before being defeated by a famous Roman soldier called Pompey. In the end, about 10,000 pirates were killed and a further 20,000 were captured.

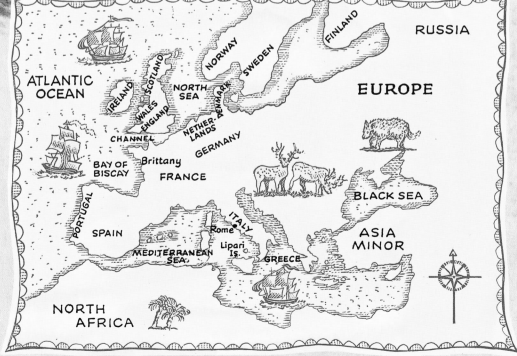

# Viking fury

 In A.D. 789 pirates from Scandinavia first attacked the coasts of the British Isles. These ancestors of today's Danes, Norwegians, and Swedes became known as Northmen or "Vikings," after their word for "sea raiding." The Vikings lived by fishing, farming, and trading. But life was hard in their northern homeland, so they sailed abroad to plunder shipping and towns.

## Enemies of God

The Vikings despised the peace-loving Christian monks of western Europe. Their abbeys and churches made easy targets. When the pirates waded ashore from their long ships, monks fled with the church treasure.

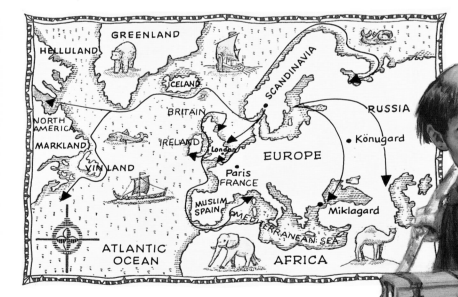

▲ The Vikings were feared far and wide for 300 years. They raided Britain, Ireland, and France. They sailed west to Iceland, Greenland, and North America, and south to the Mediterranean. They settled in Russia and sailed down the rivers of eastern Europe as far as Miklagard (now Istanbul).

◀ **Viking pirates** wore helmets made of leather or iron and carried round wooden shields. They were armed with spears, long swords, and battle-axes. Some wore mail shirts, made of iron rings.

▲ **A long ship** could be over 75 feet in length. The planks and keel were made from oak. The mast might be made of pine. It supported a broad, single sail. Holes in the planking supported the oars. The warriors rowed the ship themselves and probably sat on wooden chests. A side paddle acted as a rudder, steering the ship.

V iking warriors were called "berserkers"—they worked themselves into a battle fury, burning, killing, and looting. They also took captives and sold them as slaves. But the Vikings were not all bad—they often settled in the lands they attacked and built new towns.

## Viking plunder

Christian churches and abbeys provided the Viking pirates with valuable crosses, chalices, dishes, and bells. Raids on large towns such as London and Paris provided coins, jewelry, weapons, and bales of fine cloth. The plunder could be taken home by ship, or sold at a good profit in other countries.

# Atlantic storms

The northwestern coasts of Europe are rugged, pounded by Atlantic breakers. Small inlets, remote islands, and secret caves made ideal territory for smugglers and pirates. In the Middle Ages and beyond, piracy was common in Scotland, Ireland, Wales, the Isle of Man, the Scilly Isles, and Brittany.

### Queen of Clew Bay

Gráinne Ni Mháille, or Gráinne Mhaol, was known to the English as Grace O'Malley. This Irish noblewoman, born in about 1530, became a skilled seafarer. She had a large fleet of galleys based in Clew Bay, on Ireland's west coast. Her pirates raided the Irish coast and attacked Atlantic shipping from the 1560s. She negotiated a royal pardon in 1593 and retired.

### The devil's own

In the 1200s a Flemish monk named Eustace left his monastery to become a soldier. When he was outlawed for murder he turned pirate, working the English Channel first for the English and then the French. Eustace was beheaded in a sea battle, as this manuscript of the time shows.

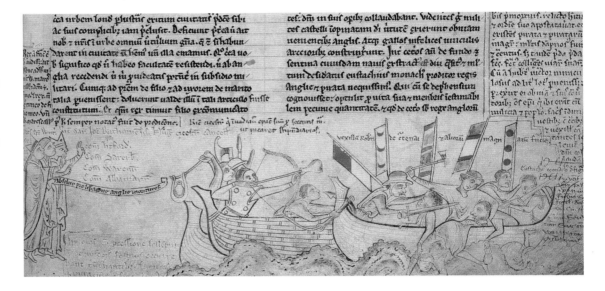

### Klein Hänslein

On a single day in 1573, 33 pirates were executed in Hamburg, Germany. Their captain was named Little Jack, or Klein Hänslein. He was the terror of merchant shipping in the North Sea.

To the east, the English Channel, North Sea, and Baltic were unsafe for shipping. These were lawless times. For many people, piracy seemed a fair way to attack enemies and rivals, or to gain wealth. Many powerful and respectable families organized pirate crews.

◀ St. Malo was already a corsair haven when Brittany came under French rule in 1488. Privateers kept up the tradition, attacking English shipping around the world. Corsair captains such as Réné Duguay-Trouin and Robert Surcouf became heroes.

The countries of Europe were often at war with each other, and it became common for seafarers to attack and plunder enemy ships. Whether they were pirates or official privateers, they all became known by the French term, corsairs. Many became popular heroes, and some played an important part in history.

## Across the English Channel

Other corsair ports on the Channel were Boulogne and Dunkirk. The most famous corsair of Dunkirk was Jean Bart. He attacked Dutch fishing vessels and raided the English coast. Captured in England in 1694, he escaped to France by rowing a small boat 150 miles across the Channel.

13

## Treasure fleets

The mainland of Central and South America was known as "the Spanish Main." This name was later used for the whole of the Caribbean. From the 1540s onward, the Spanish organized two naval convoys each year to carry all the treasure back home. One left from Vera Cruz and the other from Nombre de Dios (or later from Portobello). The two convoys joined forces off Cuba for the voyage back to Spain. The combined fleet could number up to 100 vessels. The treasure was transported in ships called galleons, which could carry 200 crew and 60 cannons. Few pirate ships could match them, but pirates had the advantage when it came to speed and cunning.

▶ In June 1523 a French corsair named Jean Fleury (or Florin) was prowling the Atlantic shipping lanes off Cape St. Vincent, near Faro in Portugal. He sighted three caravels, small three-masted vessels, bound for Spain.

Fleury closed on the ships and managed to capture two of them, although the third escaped.

14

The Spanish caravels were loaded with vast amounts of treasure seized from the Aztecs, a Native American people who lived in what is now Mexico. The powerful Aztec Empire had been defeated by a Spanish soldier, Hernando Cortés, in 1521. Fleury's attack on the Spanish treasure fleet was the first of many by French and English corsairs.

# A NEW WORLD

On October 12, 1492 an Italian seafarer, Christopher Columbus, landed on Watling's Island in the Bahamas. Columbus was in the service of the king and queen of Spain and thought he had reached part of Asia. In fact he had landed in the Americas, a "new world" unknown to Europeans. In the years that followed, Spain seized vast areas of land in the Americas.

Many Native Americans were enslaved, murdered, or died of disease. Gold and silver were shipped back to Europe. Plantations were set up on the Caribbean islands, and these were worked by poor Europeans and African slaves. This combination of desperate men, remote islands, and Spanish treasure could only lead to one thing—piracy.

▶ Francis Drake was an English privateer who often broke the rules to engage in piracy. From 1567 to 1596, he led one attack after another on the Spanish fleet, capturing a vast fortune in gold. In 1572, when England was supposed to be at peace with Spain, Drake attacked Nombre de Dios.

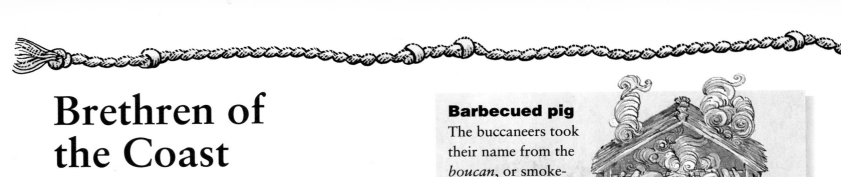

# Brethren of the Coast

In the 1600s large numbers of wild adventurers and outlaws took refuge in the Caribbean. They came from Holland, the British Isles, France, Portugal, West Africa, and from the Caribbean islands themselves. Some were known as "buccaneers," others as "Brethren of the Coast." At first they lived on Cuba, Jamaica, and Hispaniola. From the 1630s, their chief base was the island of Tortuga.

**Barbecued pig**
The buccaneers took their name from the *boucan*, or smokehouse, in which they cooked meat. Raw meat was placed over a wood-chip fire and preserved by the clouds of smoke.

▼ The buccaneers were armed with long muskets, axes, and knives. Their loose linen shirts and rough leather breeches were filthy and stank.

▶ The buccaneers lived outside the law, brawling and shooting. They were often drunk on rum and brandy. The early buccaneers lived in rough, open-air camps and hunted wild pigs and cattle with dogs. They traded the meat and hides of the animals they hunted for gunpowder and supplies.

**Roche Brasiliano**  **François l'Ollonois**  **Bartolomeo el Portugués**

### Three madmen

Some mad and violent buccaneers took pride in acts of cruelty. Roche Brasiliano, a Dutch captain, roasted his enemies alive. Jean-David Nau, a Breton better known as François l'Ollonois, hacked out the heart of a Spanish captive and tore it with his teeth. Bartolomeo the Portuguese was a notorious murderer.

The colonial governors soon had enough of the lawless buccaneers. They tried to stop their trade in cattle and pig meat, so the buccaneers decided to become pirates. By the 1660s they were launching fierce attacks on the Spanish treasure ships. This suited Spain's enemies very well. They began to hire buccaneer armies to plunder Spanish towns on the mainland. The great age of buccaneering lasted into the 1690s. The pirates' fame spread around the world.

▲ The mainland of Central and South America stayed under Spanish rule during the 1650s, but in the Caribbean, Spain's power was challenged by the British and French—and by pirates of all nations who used the islands to hide from the law.

▶ The buccaneers attacked Spanish galleons from dugout canoes, or *piraguas*. These were fast and a difficult target for enemy cannons.

# Port Royal, Jamaica

In 1655 Britain seized the Caribbean island of Jamaica from the Spanish. The newcomers did not have enough troops to hold the island against a Spanish or French attack, so they struck a deal with the buccaneers. The pirates could anchor at Port Royal and frighten off enemy shipping. The most famous buccaneer to base himself in Port Royal was a Welsh rogue named Henry Morgan. Morgan was given official backing to raid Spanish towns on the mainland.

◄ Port Royal in the 1660s became famous for its lawlessness. The smelly streets of the port were filled with drunken merchants, cruel slave traders, sailors with squawking parrots, gamblers and rogues, and swaggering buccaneers.

## Morgan's raids

Between 1668 and 1671, Henry Morgan led his men on raids against Puerto Principe, Portobello, Maracaibo, and Panama.

Henry Morgan was now a privateer who could raise large armies from among the buccaneers. Because of this, the colonial authorities in Jamaica chose to ignore his illegal acts of piracy and cruelty. He was knighted by King Charles II and was even made Lieutenant Governor of Jamaica. A heavy drinker, Morgan died in 1688. After his death the colony no longer needed its unruly buccaneers. Indeed, Port Royal now became famous as the place where pirates were captured, tried, and hanged.

## God's punishment?

On June 7, 1692 the busy streets and wharves of Port Royal suddenly fell silent. And then the whole earth shook and rumbled. Taverns collapsed and warehouses packed with sugar and tobacco fell into the harbor. The sea flooded into the town. As news of the earthquake spread, people claimed that Port Royal was being punished for its sins.

## Women pirates

Three pirates were among many brought to trial in Jamaica in November 1720. One, John Rackham, was found guilty and hanged. The other two were found guilty, but were let off—when the court found that they were both expecting babies. Their names were Mary Read and Anne Bonny. Read and Bonny had been brought up as boys, so they were used to dressing in men's clothes and found them better suited to life at sea. They fought violently with cutlasses, axes, and pistols, and became the best known women pirates of all time.

◄ John Rackham was known as "Calico Jack" because he wore brightly colored clothes made of calico, a type of cotton. In 1719 Calico Jack came to New Providence Island, in the Bahamas, and took up with Anne Bonny. They stole a sloop and sailed off to a life of crime. Rackham captured Mary Read, and she joined up with his pirate crew.

# North American waters

While the Spanish ruled the Caribbean and the Pacific coasts, British colonists settled along the eastern coast of North America. They had to pay high taxes to the government back home for many of the goods they imported. In the 1700s some settlers got their revenge by taking up smuggling and piracy. They preyed on shipping from Newfoundland down to the Carolinas, and often even farther away. Some colonial governors could be persuaded to take no notice, provided they were given a share of the profits.

### Down in New Orleans

Jean Lafitte was a notorious pirate and smuggler who controlled every racket in New Orleans. When the United States went to war against Britain in 1812, Lafitte turned down an offer of money from the British. Instead he offered his services to the Americans and became a privateer— and a hero.

### Stede Bonnet

Stede Bonnet was a respectable, middle-aged gentleman who had a reputation as a dandy. He had retired from the army and owned a plantation in Barbados. Feeling depressed, or perhaps just bored with life, Bonnet turned pirate captain. For a time he sailed with Blackbeard's fleet, where he became a figure of fun. In 1718 Bonnet was captured and hanged in Charleston.

After Port Royal was cleaned up, Nassau on New Providence Island in the Bahamas attracted thousands of pirates. They lived riotously and joined the attack on Atlantic shipping. In 1775 war broke out between Great Britain and her American colonies. The Americans had only a small navy, so they relied on privateers to attack British merchant ships. By 1783 the Americans had trounced the British and formed an independent nation—the United States.

### Blackbeard's terror

The most feared pirate in North America from 1716 onward was English-born Edward Teach, known as "Blackbeard." He was a brutal man who wore his hair and beard in long braided "dreadlocks." He tied smoldering fuses under his hat to terrify his victims.

▶ In November 1718 Governor Alexander Spotswood of Virginia offered £100—then a huge sum—for the capture of Blackbeard. Lieutenant Robert Maynard of HMS *Pearl* killed the pirate in a desperate hand-to-hand fight. He cut off Blackbeard's head and hung it from the bowsprit.

# COASTS OF AFRICA

Most of Africa remained unknown to the outside world until the 1800s. Medieval maps were often left blank or covered with pictures of lions. Rich empires existed inland, but few explorers survived the long journeys through deserts and jungles to reach them.

▼ The Welsh pirate captain Bartholomew Roberts checks his haul of treasure by the Senegal River in 1721. Roberts was one of the most successful pirates of all time, capturing or sinking over 400 ships.

## Black Bart

Bartholomew "Black Bart" Roberts served under a Welsh pirate named Howell Davis. When Davis was killed in 1719, Roberts was elected captain. He loved fine clothes and lived in style. He is said to have preferred tea to rum, but his crew was drunk when a British anti-piracy ship, HMS *Swallow*, discovered them anchored in the lee of Cape Lopez. Roberts was shot in the throat.

The African coasts were charted from the Middle Ages onward by Europeans, Arabs, and Chinese traders. The first Europeans to reach the Gulf of Guinea were the Portuguese, who built forts and trading posts. They were followed in the 1500s and 1600s by other Europeans who were greedy for gold and ivory. They soon turned to another, crueler, trade—kidnapping Africans and transporting them to the New World as slaves. By the 1700s the Guinea Coast was plagued by pirates too, who were eager to make their own profits out of so much human misery.

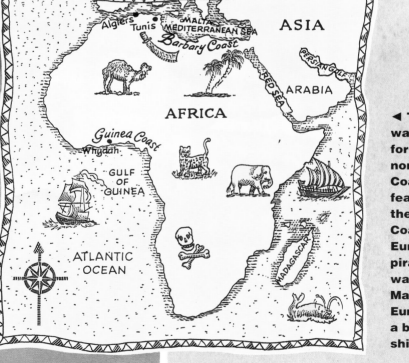

◄ The African coastline was the haunt of pirates for many centuries. In the north was the Barbary Coast, home of the much-feared Muslim corsairs. In the west, the Guinea Coast was raided by European slavers and pirates. In the southeast was the island of Madagascar, which European pirates used as a base for their raids on ships in the Indian Ocean.

# Barbary corsairs

Arab Muslims first invaded North Africa in the 640s. Within 100 years their rule stretched to southern Spain. During the 1530s most of North Africa came under Turkish Muslim rule, but southern Europe remained Christian. Muslim corsairs from Tripoli, Tunis, and Algiers—all on the Berber, or Barbary, Coast—raided European shipping and captured Christian crews as slaves.

**Torture**
Christian prisoners of the Barbary corsairs were shown little mercy, unless they were rich. They were chained, flogged with knotted ropes, and tortured. Muslim prisoners in Christian jails were also treated with great cruelty.

▼ Barbary corsairs used fast galleys rowed by slaves. The galleys were commanded by a sea captain, or *raïs*, and contained crack troops. This painting by Cornelius Vroom shows a battle between corsairs and Spanish ships in 1615.

## The Redemptionists

Christian priests called Redemptionists (buyers back) raised funds for Christians enslaved by the corsairs. They visited the Barbary Coast and paid off the ransoms demanded by the Muslim rulers.

Barbary corsairs were soon carrying out raids far from Africa, even sailing to Iceland. They became heroes of the Islamic world. In the 1600s many Europeans "turned Turk" and joined the Barbary corsairs. These included Englishman Sir Francis Verney and Dutchmen Simon Danziger and Jan Jansz. Christian corsairs in their turn built fleets to attack the Muslims. They were based on the Mediterranean island of Malta.

## The Barbarossas

The most famous leaders of the early Barbary corsairs were two brothers called Aruj and Kheir-ed-Din. Born in Greece, they became known as the Barbarossa (red beard) brothers.

▼ In 1504 Aruj Barbarossa captured two treasure galleys owned by Pope Julius II. The Barbarossa brothers were skilled seamen and fierce fighters. They went on to attack the Genoese and the Spanish, who killed Aruj in 1518.

Kheir-ed-Din became a respected admiral and ambassador.

# Pirate kingdoms

Other African coasts were notorious centers of piracy. In the 1600s Dutch, French, and Portuguese pirates cruised the shores of southern Africa. Soon pirates were sailing all the way from North America to Africa and up the Red Sea—a route that became known as "the Pirate Round." From 1690 until 1720, the pirates' chief base was Madagascar. Rumors spread about the easy life to be had on the island, about the beautiful women and tropical sunshine. But the life led by Madagascar pirates was really a tough one.

▲ This map shows Madagascar, chief port of call on the Pirate Round. The island became a place where pirates took on food and water or sold cargoes they had captured in the Indian Ocean.

## A kind pirate

Pirate captains were not often known for their kindness. The Irish pirate Edward England operated on the Guinea Coast and in the Indian Ocean. But when he let a British merchant captain sail off unharmed, England's crew was disgusted and dumped him in Mauritius. He built a small boat and rowed all the way to Madagascar.

▼ Careening took place when a ship was beached for repairs. This was the moment when pirates were most at risk from attack. They camped on the shore and had no means of escape.

In tropical waters the hulls of wooden ships soon became covered with barnacles and seaweed and were riddled with holes made by marine worms. Pirates stopped at St. Mary's Island, off Madagascar, to repair their ships.

Daniel Defoe (1661–1731) wrote of a new country called Libertalia, founded on Madagascar by a pirate named Captain Misson. It probably never existed, but other Madagascar pirates did declare themselves local rulers. There was "King" Abraham Samuel in the 1690s and James Plantain, "King of Ranter Bay," in the 1720s.

## Tools of the trade

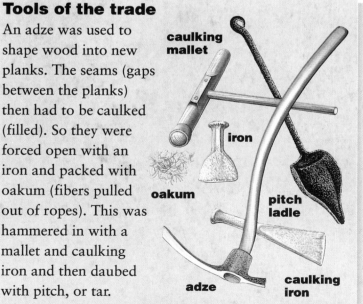

An adze was used to shape wood into new planks. The seams (gaps between the planks) then had to be caulked (filled). So they were forced open with an iron and packed with oakum (fibers pulled out of ropes). This was hammered in with a mallet and caulking iron and then daubed with pitch, or tar.

caulking mallet

iron

oakum

pitch ladle

adze

caulking iron

# EASTERN MENACE

In 1735 the *Derby*, a ship belonging to the British East India Company, was forced to surrender to the Angria family, a group of seafarers who raided shipping on the west coast of India. On board was a fortune in gold, bound for the port of Bombay.

▶ Crew on board the *Derby* warn of Angria vessels coming closer. The Angria family belonged to the Maratha people, who were challenging the trading rights of the Company. The Marathas controlled the Malabar Coast, the waters south of Bombay, and built a chain of forts along the shore.

▲ The Persian Gulf and the Arabian Sea link Europe and southwest Asia with India and the Far East. This is one of the richest trading routes in the world. In these waters, piracy has been a problem that is as old as trading itself.

The British East India Company was founded in 1600 to trade in the Indian and Pacific oceans. It had its own soldiers and sailors. Its ships were called East Indiamen, and during the 1700s they were often attacked by the Marathas. The first great leader of the Maratha attacks was Kanhoji Angria, who died in 1729.

### The Malabar coast

The Malabar coast was the name given to the western Indian waters south of Bombay. The area was controlled by the Marathas, who built a chain of forts along the shore. In 1756 they were finally defeated.

# Red Sea, red blood

European trade with India and the Far East grew and grew. The Portuguese attacked and won Goa, in India, in 1510. By the 1700s the British and French were fighting each other for control of trade with the rest of India, and the Dutch were in control of many of the "Spice Islands" of Southeast Asia. The European powers authorized privateers to attack one another's trade. Privateering soon turned into out-and-out piracy.

**Long Ben**
Englishman Henry Avery was known as "Long Ben" or "Captain Bridgeman." He became so famous that people called him "the Arch-Pirate." Avery made a fortune from piracy in the Red Sea, but lost it all and seems to have died in poverty at home in Devon.

**The *Gang-i-Sawai***
In September 1695 Avery and pirates from North America attacked the chief vessel of the Moghul fleet, the *Gang-i-Sawai*. On board were pilgrims returning from the holy city of Mecca, and vast treasure.

▶ After two hours of fighting, pirates from Avery's ship, the *Fancy*, swarmed onto the *Gang-i-Sawai* and attacked the Moghul women who were on board.

Pirate crews set out from Europe and the colonies of North America. They sailed northward from Madagascar into the Arabian Sea, the Persian Gulf, and the Red Sea, where they attacked European merchant ships. The pirate ships were often secretly sponsored by rich and powerful backers. They shared the spoils with the crew if the trip was successful and pleaded ignorance if the crew was caught.

The pirates also attacked the ships of Aurangzeb, the Moghul emperor who ruled a large part of northern India from 1658 until 1707. Europeans at that time had little respect for people who were not Christians, and pirates who attacked Muslim shipping often escaped justice.

## Voyage of disaster

Scottish-born William Kidd lived in New York City. He was given a royal commission to attack French shipping and pirates in the Indian Ocean, but was forced by his crew to take up more profitable piracy. In October 1697 he argued with his gunner William Moore and killed him with a blow from a bucket. Kidd was arrested and hanged.

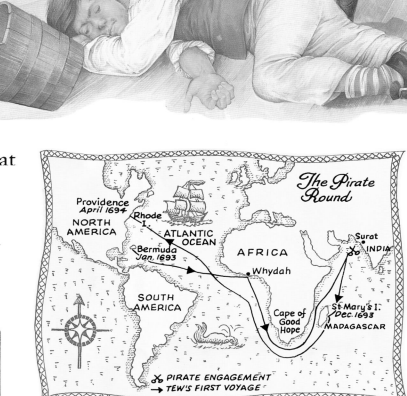

▲ The Pirate Round could involve a voyage of about 24,000 miles. Thomas Tew sailed with the *Amity* from Bermuda to Whydah, on the Guinea Coast, and turned pirate in the Indian Ocean. He then sailed back to his home on Rhode Island and bribed the authorities to ignore his crimes. He returned to the Indian Ocean and joined up with Henry Avery, but was shot and killed in 1695.

# Far Eastern seas

The Chinese were some of the greatest shipbuilders of the ancient world. They were the first to design ships with several masts and with large underwater rudders. They also invented the compass. Chinese fleets of wooden sailing ships, called junks, explored the Indian Ocean in the 1400s. The Chinese were skillful traders—and pirates.

▲ The South China Sea was infested with pirates from the Middle Ages until well into the 1900s.

To the south, the Strait of Malacca and the Java Sea were just as dangerous.

◄ In September 1849 a Chinese pirate fleet based at Bias Bay, to the east of Hong Kong, was attacked and destroyed by British warships. Over 400 pirates were killed. Their leader, Cui Apu, was wounded. He escaped but was later betrayed. He committed suicide in 1851.

## Japanese pirates and Kublai Khan

In the 1270s Japanese pirates raided the Chinese coast, attacking villages and ships. The ruler of China, Kublai Khan, complained to Japan. Nothing was done, so he decided to invade Japan. His two attempts, in 1274 and 1281, were both foiled by storms at sea.

▲ Japanese pirate ship

## Borneo bandits

The island of Borneo has many rivers and creeks fringed by dense forests. For hundreds of years these were the haunt of Dayak pirates, who were fierce headhunters. They attacked shipping from light, speedy boats called *prahus*. In the 1840s the Dayak pirates were ruthlessly hunted down by the British navy.

▲ Dayak pirate

## To the Philippines

The islands of the Sulu Sea were havens for local pirates and slavers. Farther east again were the dreaded Ilanun pirates of Mindanão, who made long sea voyages in search of booty. As the Europeans took over their trade in the 1800s, many Southeast Asian peoples were driven to desperate measures such as piracy in order to survive.

▲ Ilanun pirate

## The dragon lady

By the 1800s the coasts around the port of Canton were controlled by the fleets of a Chinese pirate named Cheng I. When he died in 1807 his widow Madame Cheng took his place. She soon controlled one of the largest and deadliest pirate fleets in history, with 800 armed junks, 1,000 smaller boats, and over 70,000 men and women under her ruthless command. After battles with rival pirates, she bought her pardon from the Chinese government in 1810.

Seafarers in the Far East faced many dangers, from typhoons to sharks. But their chief fear was of Chinese pirates. The pirate fleets were large and well organized, often made up of political rebels and outlaws. They attacked both Chinese and European shipping and treated their prisoners with great cruelty. The pirates of the Spice Islands far to the south were also much feared.

1 mainmast
2 mizzenmast
3 quarterdeck
4 captain's cabin
5 rudder
6 food stores
7 frames
8 keel
9 magazine

10 sail locker
11 capstan
12 pumps
13 bilges
14 shot locker
15 water supply
16 ship's stores
17 oars
18 hull

19 foc's'le (forecastle)
20 anchor
21 bowsprit
22 foremast
23 bell
24 cannon
25 galley (kitchen)
26 gun deck
27 gunwale
28 lantern

▼ While Captain Kidd slept in the Great Cabin, his crew of about 150 men slept below decks.

▼ The 34 cannons used 12-pound cannonballs. The shot locker stored up to six tons of ammunition.

▲ The casks of drinking water weighed a ton each and also served as ballast, keeping the ship stable. When the casks were empty, the crew went ashore to refill them at fresh springs.

▲ While not in use, the sails were stored away from sea spray in a dry locker, so that they would not rot.

▲ Meat was salted down and preserved in barrels. But it often went rotten and hungry crews would catch fish or go ashore to hunt for fresh meat.

▲ The gunpowder store (magazine) was vital to any pirate ship. The smallest spark could blow it up at any time.

▲ The bilges below decks were full of foul, slopping water. The ship's pumps helped keep the boat dry and afloat.

▲ The ship was steered by a huge wooden rudder linked to the ship's wheel.

◄ The galley was a simple wood-burning range, built for safety well away from the gunpowder store.

► Thick cables called forestays were tied to the bowsprit to support the foremast.

Speed and surprise were always the keys to success as a pirate. The buccaneers of the Caribbean soon found out that with small, fast vessels they could easily outwit a slow, lumbering galleon, however heavily it was armed. The French corsairs often used small armed fishing boats to attack English shipping.

Pirates down on their luck might have to use a leaky old tub, but they could always try to capture or steal the very latest in naval design. Many pirate ships were naval or privateering vessels that had been seized by the crew during a mutiny.

Old sailing ships needed constant maintenance and hard work to keep them going. Shipwrecks were common.

▲ The oars were used when there was no wind, or when the ship was entering a port.

## The *Adventure Galley*

This was the ship that took Captain William Kidd on an ill-fated voyage in 1696. It was built the year before on the Thames River at Deptford, near London. The ship was 125 feet long and was designed for privateering. It was powered by wind and sail, but if the wind failed the ship could be rowed with 32 oars. Each oar was pulled by two or more men.

Kidd's crew was a bunch of murderous thugs who had been press-ganged into joining up. They forced him to take up piracy. The ship had problems with leaks, and in the end Kidd had to abandon the *Galley*.

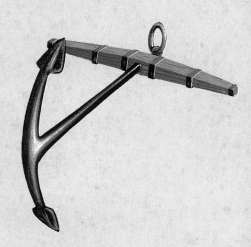

► The anchor of the *Adventure Galley* weighed nearly 3,000 pounds. Its heavy cable could only be raised with a capstan, which was pushed around and around by the muscle power of the crew. Singing or fiddle music helped the crew to keep the right rhythm and timing.

# Sails and rigging

The *Adventure Galley* could carry up to 28,000 square feet of sail, which gave it a top speed of about 14 knots (16 miles per hour). Sails were made of very tough canvas called "sailcloth," woven from hemp, cotton, or linen. They often had to stand up to gales and hurricanes, so extra sections of sailcloth were stitched on to make the sails tougher.

▼ The *Adventure Galley* was a square-rigged ship. Its square sails were supported by crossbars called yards.

1 sprit topsail
2 spritsail
3 spritsail course
4 inner jib
5 outer jib
6 fore topgallant
7 fore topsail
8 fore top
9 foresail
10 main topgallant
11 main topsail
12 main top
13 mainsail
14 mizzen topgallant
15 mizzen topsail
16 mizzen top
17 spanker
18 yard

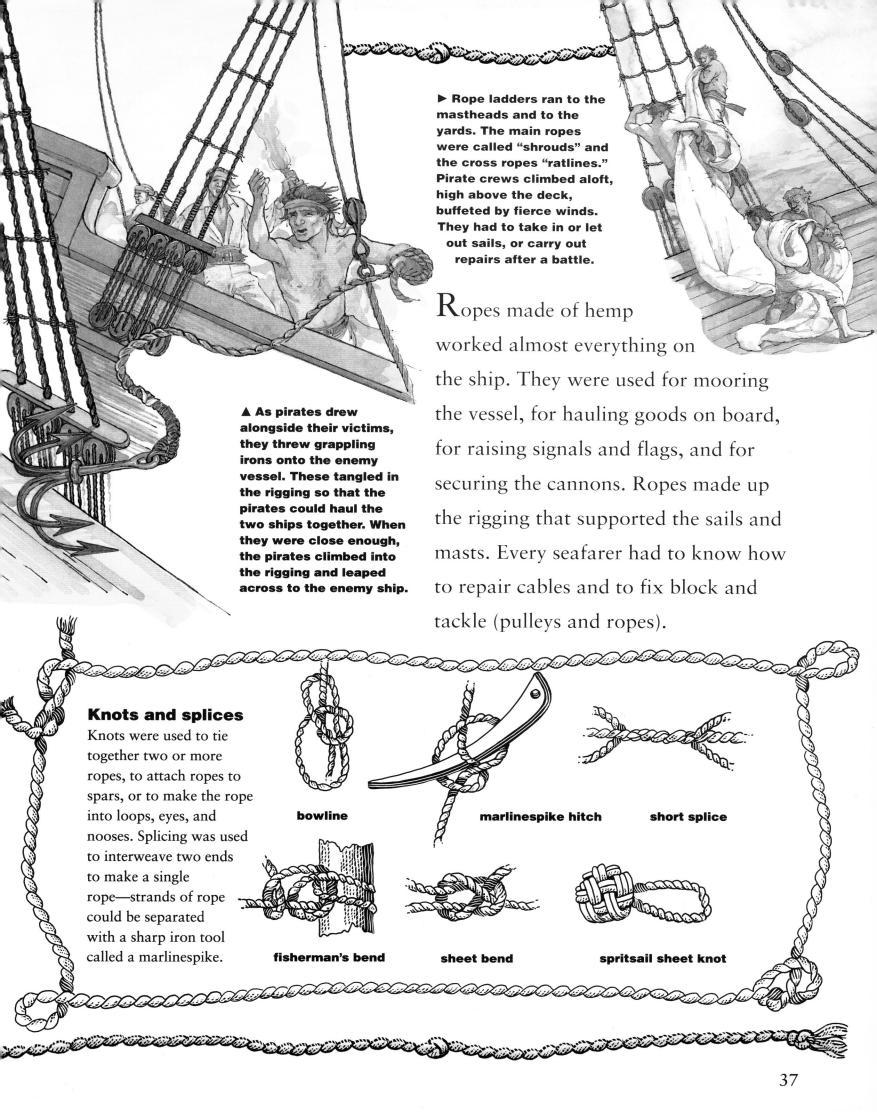

► Rope ladders ran to the mastheads and to the yards. The main ropes were called "shrouds" and the cross ropes "ratlines." Pirate crews climbed aloft, high above the deck, buffeted by fierce winds. They had to take in or let out sails, or carry out repairs after a battle.

▲ As pirates drew alongside their victims, they threw grappling irons onto the enemy vessel. These tangled in the rigging so that the pirates could haul the two ships together. When they were close enough, the pirates climbed into the rigging and leaped across to the enemy ship.

Ropes made of hemp worked almost everything on the ship. They were used for mooring the vessel, for hauling goods on board, for raising signals and flags, and for securing the cannons. Ropes made up the rigging that supported the sails and masts. Every seafarer had to know how to repair cables and to fix block and tackle (pulleys and ropes).

## Knots and splices

Knots were used to tie together two or more ropes, to attach ropes to spars, or to make the rope into loops, eyes, and nooses. Splicing was used to interweave two ends to make a single rope—strands of rope could be separated with a sharp iron tool called a marlinespike.

**bowline**

**marlinespike hitch**

**short splice**

**fisherman's bend**

**sheet bend**

**spritsail sheet knot**

# Through the ages

The size and design of pirate ships varied greatly from age to age and from one part of the world to another. By the 1800s sailing ships were faster and more streamlined than ever. This may have helped the pirates, but it also helped the pirate chasers. Soon navies had powerful steamships armed with modern guns to hunt down the pirates.

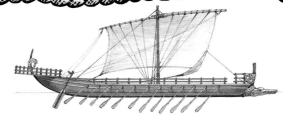

**Greek pirate galley, 500 B.C.**
These galleys had oars and a single sail. They were much faster than merchant ships laden with goods.

**English nef, 1400**
Pirates went into battle on ships with high fighting decks called "castles" at each end.

**English galleon, 1580**
Many of Queen Elizabeth I's sea captains engaged in piracy as well as privateering.

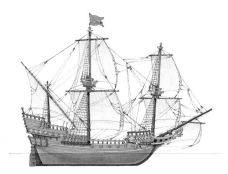

**Dutch East Indiaman, 1700**
Merchant vessels trading with Southeast Asia faced attacks from pirates and privateers.

**Galley, 1715**
English galleys traded in slaves and sugar in the Americas and were rich prizes for pirates.

**Pirate sloop, Nassau, 1720**
American sloops were speedy, single-masted ships with a fore-and-aft rig, ideal for the pirates of the Bahamas.

**British man-o'-war, 1815**
Heavily armed warships like these were used to fight piracy in the Arabian Sea.

**Chinese pirate junk, 1845**
This three-masted junk was 80 feet long and had a large rudder. It carried 30 cannons.

**Paddle-steamer, 1870**
Steamships helped the European countries stamp out piracy in Southeast Asia.

### Roman pirate chaser, 70 B.C.

This warship used against Cilician pirates was a trireme, a galley with three banks of oars.

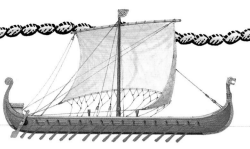

### Viking long ship, A.D. 900

Simple but deadly, the long ship carried a crew of up to 50 men. It had long oars and a single sail.

### Arab dhow, A.D. 900

This classic ship design is still in use today. The triangular sail is called a "lateen."

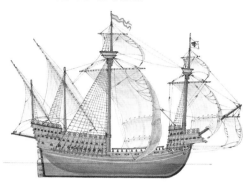

### Spanish galleon, 1580

This heavily armed Spanish treasure ship was rather clumsy in battle.

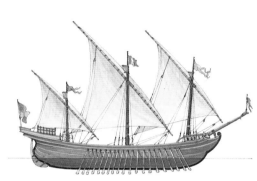

### Barbary corsair, 1660

These Muslim galleys from North Africa were rowed by captured Christians who were slaves.

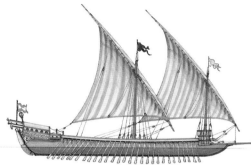

### Maltese corsair, 1660

Galleys from Malta attacked the Barbary corsairs. They were rowed by Muslim slaves.

**Note: These pirate ships, privateers, merchant vessels, and pirate chasers are not shown to scale.**

### Topsail schooner, 1812

American privateers used these beautiful two-masted vessels to raid British shipping.

### British gunship, 1900

By the 1900s few pirates could challenge the power of modern gunship patrols.

Steel and steam replaced wood and sail, and with the coming of radio, few remote islands or lonely coasts were beyond the reach of the law.

**Bartholomew Roberts (Black Bart)**

**Christopher Moody**

**Edward Teach (Blackbeard)**

**Henry Avery (Long Ben)**

**John Rackham (Calico Jack)**

**Thomas Tew**

**Christopher Condent**

Pirate flags were meant to strike fear into the enemy. They often showed skulls, swords, crossbones, devils, and hearts.

# Blackjacks and spyglasses

 The first pirate flags were blood red. They were hoisted before battle to signal that no one would be spared. It is thought that the French words *joli rouge* (pretty red) became the "Jolly Roger"—the English term for any pirate flag. In the 1690s and 1700s many pirate captains designed their own flags. They were white on a field of red or, more often, black. These came to be known as "blackjacks."

▲ This beautiful flag was captured from Chinese pirates in 1849. They believed it brought good luck and calm seas.

Chinese pirate fleets were divided into battle groups. Each one flew under a different colored flag.

Pirates had to keep a lookout for other vessels all the time. One pirate would climb the main top to look for distant sails on the horizon. The captain would shout out orders to the crew on the quarterdeck if the ship's course had to be changed. The Welsh pirate Howell Davis often used flags to fool his enemies. He flew an English or French flag, or forced vessels he had just defeated to fly a length of black cloth— so that pursuing ships thought they faced a large pirate fleet.

chart

compass

backstaff

dividers

telescope

### Finding the way
Navigation is the science of finding the way at sea. A ship's compass has a needle that swings to the north and shows in which direction the ship is sailing. Charts show coastlines, sandbanks, currents, and tides. Dividers are used to measure distances on a chart. With a telescope, or "spyglass," a sailor can identify another ship's flag or sight land.

▼ **This pirate holds the ship on course, turning the wheel to move the rudder. He checks the compass mounted in front of the wheel.**

▼ **His shipmate spies the flag of an enemy through the telescope.**

▲ **A backstaff is used to find the ship's position in relation to the sun. The navigator stands with his back to the sun and measures its shadow.**

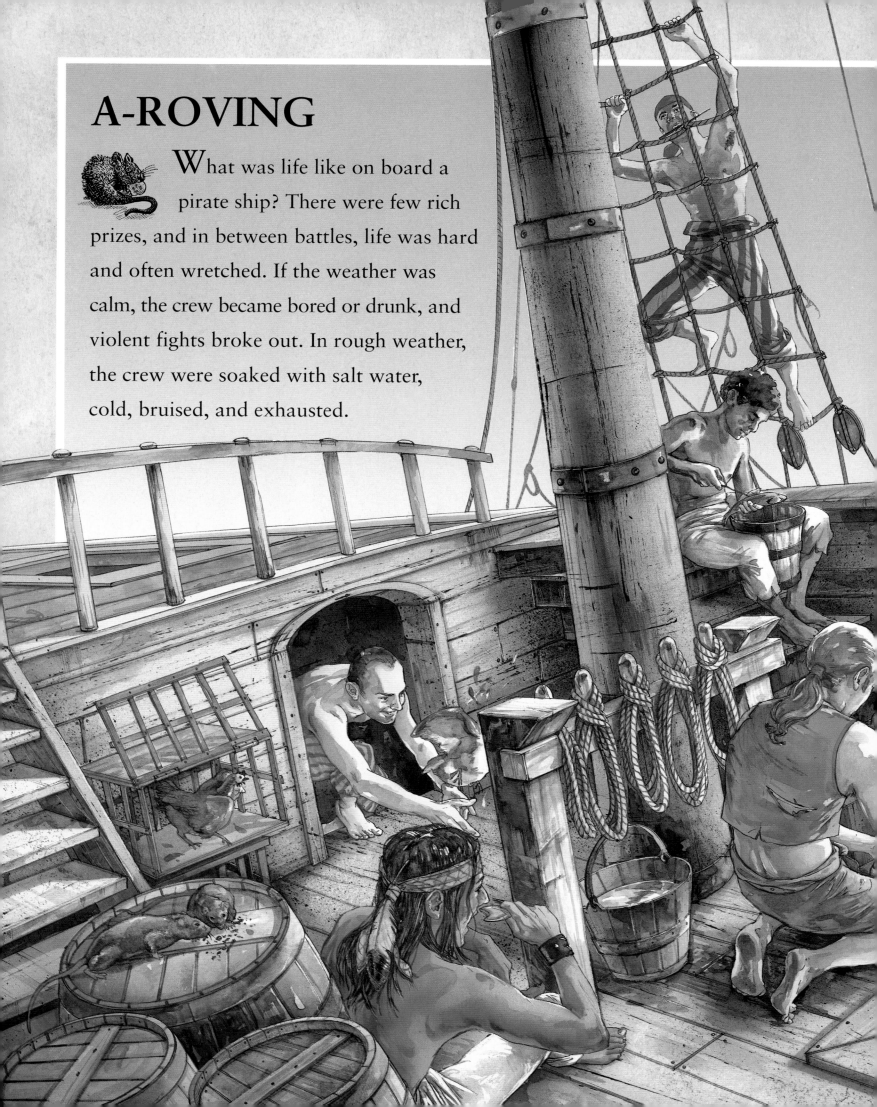

# A-ROVING

What was life like on board a pirate ship? There were few rich prizes, and in between battles, life was hard and often wretched. If the weather was calm, the crew became bored or drunk, and violent fights broke out. In rough weather, the crew were soaked with salt water, cold, bruised, and exhausted.

▼ These pirates are on the main deck by the galley. One pirate relaxes with a pipe, while another gnaws at "hardtack," the ship's biscuits that were eaten on most long voyages. The biscuits were nearly always stale and full of wriggling weevils. Meat was dried or salted and in short supply. Chickens were kept on board for their eggs, and fish and turtles could be caught over the side of the ship. There were often periods when supplies of fresh water were low. Shipwreck could lead to starvation or even cannibalism among the survivors.

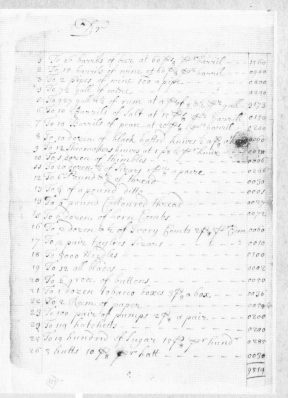

## The logbook

A ship's speed was measured by throwing a log of wood attached to a piece of string overboard and observing what length of string ran out within a given time. Captains recorded daily progress in an official "logbook." This included other details of daily events during the voyage, such as which crew members had died or been punished.

At night the pirates who were not on watch slept on the cramped lower decks. This was a dark, closed world, creaking, pitching, and tossing. Bilge water slopped below, and rats were everywhere —Chinese pirates liked to eat them. By day the tropical sun could scorch the skin. If pirates were ill, there were no medicines. Limbs injured in battle were sawn off without any anesthetic, often by the ship's carpenter. For most pirates, the only pleasures were gambling with dice or drinking rum.

▶ Pirates ate little fresh fruit or vegetables at sea and often suffered from scurvy. In 1753 James Lind discovered that eating fruit such as limes could prevent the disease. The explorer Captain Cook was the first to take Lind's advice and included limes in his crew's diet.

# "On the account"

Becoming a pirate was called "going on the account." Piracy was big business. It may have been criminal and violent, but it was also very organized. Contracts were drawn up between backers and pirate captains. The crews worked out how to divide the spoils and behaved by strict rules. Breaking them could mean a flogging, or even death.

▲ Privateer captains like William Kidd were issued with official documents called "letters of marque." These set out the terms for attacking enemy shipping without being accused of piracy.

◄ A wealthy merchant draws up a secret agreement with a pirate captain in a New York tavern. The expenses of a pirate expedition were high, but the rewards could be great.

▶ A pirate who broke the rules faced severe penalties from his shipmates. He was sometimes "marooned," or abandoned on a remote desert island. He was left with fresh water, some weapons, and gunpowder.

### Insurance claims

Just as pirates agreed to obey their captain and follow the rules, the captain and any backers of the expedition were expected to pay pirates for any injuries they received in battle. A finger or an eye lost in a sword fight might be worth a compensation award of 100 silver pieces. A whole limb shot away by cannons might be worth 600 silver pieces.

Rules and agreements were drawn up throughout the history of piracy. Pirate crews often voted on which course of action to follow. They saw themselves as free men, making their own decisions in a way that regular sailors could not.

The pirates often made very harsh decisions. If they captured a naval officer under whom they had served, they would treat him with great cruelty. "Walking the plank," often referred to in storybooks, was not a common punishment, but prisoners were often tortured or killed and thrown to the sharks.

# Fighting dirty

Stolen weapons were as valuable as any treasure to a pirate crew. The buccaneers of the Caribbean liked to swagger around with cutlasses and pistols. They used them against one another as much as against the enemy. Blackbeard once shot his first mate, Israel Hands, under the table and smashed his kneecap. As outlaws, pirates had nothing to lose by fighting to the death. When Blackbeard was finally cornered, it took five shots and 20 cutlass wounds to kill him.

## Fire and smoke

In ancient Asia and Europe, a blazing mixture of oil and tar was squirted at enemy ships. It was known as "Greek fire." The Chinese invented gunpowder about 1,000 years ago, and by the 1300s it was being used to fire primitive cannons. These often blew up, killing the gunners instead of the enemy. The cannons used by the pirates of the 1600s and 1700s were much more reliable. Pirates also made their own firebombs and hand grenades.

## Cutthroat weapons

Throughout history, pirates simply used whatever weapons they could lay their hands on. In the Middle Ages, the English Channel pirates might go into battle with boat hooks and simple knives. A gentleman pirate of the 1720s might have a set of the finest pistols. The most famous pirate weapon was the cutlass. It was a simple short-bladed slashing sword of razor-sharp steel.

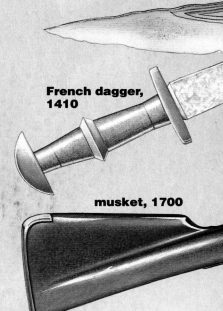

**French dagger, 1410**

**musket, 1700**

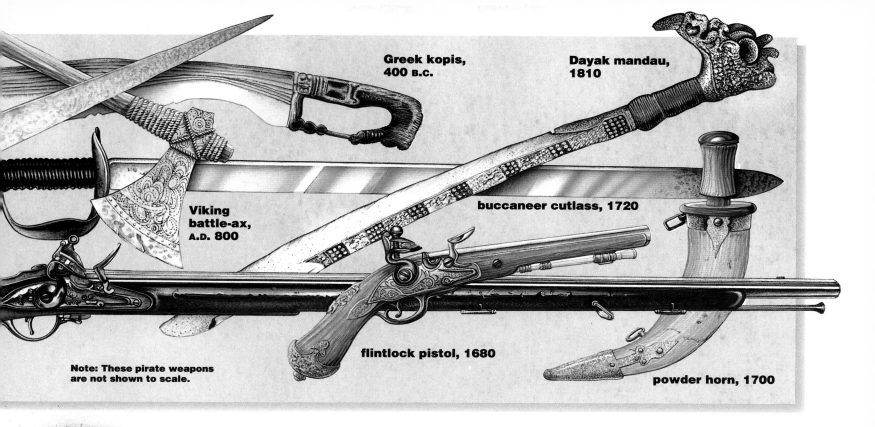

Greek kopis,
400 B.C.

Dayak mandau,
1810

Viking
battle-ax,
A.D. 800

buccaneer cutlass, 1720

flintlock pistol, 1680

powder horn, 1700

Note: These pirate weapons
are not shown to scale.

◀ Large cannons were mounted on wheeled bases. The charge of gunpowder was rammed down the barrel. The shot was then loaded and the fuse was lit. When the gun fired, it recoiled backward with great force, held by ropes. When the shot hit the enemy vessel, it brought masts and spars crashing down and sent splinters flying in all directions.

Many of the rules drawn up by pirate crews referred to personal weapons. The pirates were expected to keep their arms in working order, ready for action at all times. That meant keeping muskets cleaned and gunpowder dry, even when fighting in rough seas or tropical storms.

The long-barreled muskets and pistols used by the buccaneer sharp-shooters in the 1660s were unreliable, hard to aim, and slow to reload. As the fight closed in, the pirates fought hand to hand with cutlasses, daggers, and axes. They lashed out violently, kicking, punching, and biting.

# Pirate treasure

**W**hat did pirates dream about? Gold and silver was desired by them all, from the Cilicians of the Mediterranean to the Elizabethan rovers on the Spanish Main. It might take the form of bars, plate, goblets, or church crosses, or it might be made into coins. Precious metals, jewelry, and fancy weapons could be easily transported and sold. Cargoes such as sugar or tobacco also found a ready market. Spices from the hold of a Dutch East Indiaman were valuable but had to be dumped if no buyer could be found.

▲ Pirate crews divided up the booty, as agreed in their contract. The spoils could add up to $230,000 or more—many millions at today's values.

Some captains tried to cheat their crew by sailing off before the treasure could be divvied up.

▶ There are few records of buried treasure or secret maps. Pirates may have come ashore by night to hide their treasure on remote islands. They may also have used the old smugglers' trick of anchoring barrels of contraband to the seabed by weighting them with stones.

## Pieces-of-eight

Coins minted on the Spanish Main were sent back to Europe with the treasure fleets. They included doubloons and eight-reale pieces.

*Reale* is Spanish for "royal," but the buccaneers called them "pieces-of-eight." These types of coin stayed in use in the Caribbean for many years.

In a raid, pirates took anything they could use, including weapons, tools, medical chests, flags, ropes, and sails. They often took the whole ship, forcing its crew to join theirs. Ships that were of no use might be sunk, or "scuttled." This was done by a privateer's first mate named David Jones, in the 1630s. From then on, anything sent to the seabed was said to be "sent to Davy Jones's locker."

## Hidden hoards

Treasure hunters may never have found chests full of gold hidden *by* pirates, but they have often found hoards hidden *from* pirates. Wealthy Romans in Britain hid their valuables from Saxon pirates. Monks buried church treasure in case the Vikings got hold of it. On the Spanish Main, priests covered a gold altar in white paint—so that Morgan's buccaneers would think it was wood.

49

# A pirate's death

Few pirates lived to enjoy their wealth. Some, such as the English corsair Sir Henry Mainwaring, gained a royal pardon and abandoned piracy. Most pirates died in distant lands, in brutal battles. Thomas Tew was shot during an attack on the Mogul ship *Fateh Muhammad* in 1695. Thomas Anstis was killed in the Caribbean in about 1723, murdered by his own crew. John Ward, who turned Barbary corsair under the name "Yusuf Raïs," died of plague in Tunis in 1622. The ones who made it home, like Henry Avery, often died penniless and forgotten.

### Death of William Marsh

William de Marisco, or Marsh, was a pirate based on the island of Lundy, in the Bristol Channel. He was captured in 1242 and taken to London. There he was hauled through the streets, hanged, quartered (chopped into four pieces), and burned.

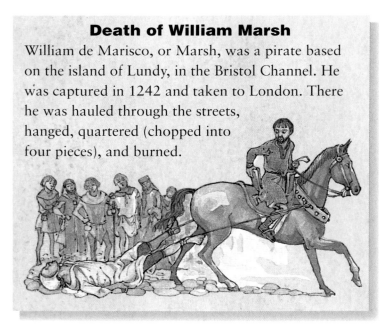

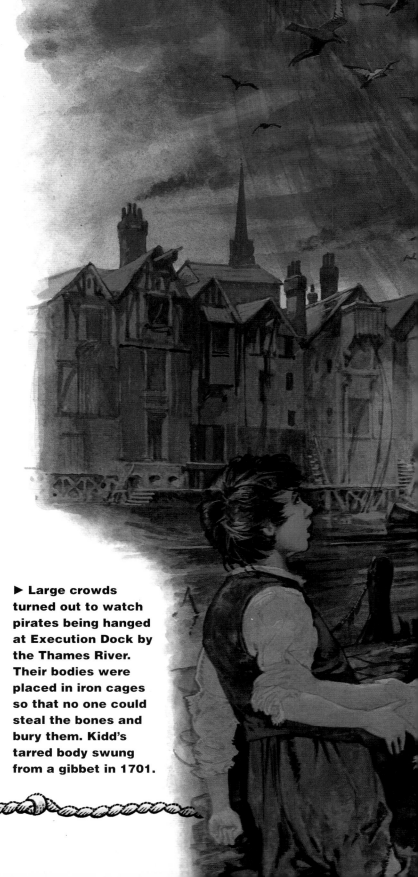

► Large crowds turned out to watch pirates being hanged at Execution Dock by the Thames River. Their bodies were placed in iron cages so that no one could steal the bones and bury them. Kidd's tarred body swung from a gibbet in 1701.

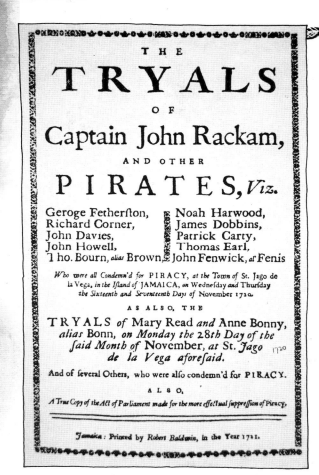

▲ **Everyone wanted to read reports of the trial of John Rackham (Calico Jack), Anne Bonny, and Mary Read. In the 1700s, popular songs were written about such pirates and their evil deeds.**

From earliest times, laws against piracy were savage. Captured pirates were tortured and enslaved. The Romans nailed pirates to crosses. The German pirate Störtebeker had his head cut off in Hamburg in 1402. English pirates of the 1700s were hanged at Execution Dock in London. The tide was allowed to wash over their bodies, which were then tarred and hung in chains as a warning to all—piracy never pays.

# CHANGING TIMES

The European pirates who terrorized the oceans between the 1500s and the 1800s were fighting at a time when Europe was trying to control the rest of the world and build up big empires overseas. Some pirates preyed off the new empires. Others, such as Henry Morgan, helped to create them.

▼ On November 13, 1809, the pirate base at Ra's al Khayma, on the Persian Gulf, was destroyed by a British taskforce. Piracy was soon under threat around the world.

▲ These captured Chinese pirates were photographed on board a British naval patrol vessel. The fight against pirates in the South China Sea lasted from the 1840s until the 1920s.

By the mid-1800s this long period of piracy was coming to an end. Britain and several other European nations now ruled most of the world. They controlled trade, and they had the most powerful guns and ships. The bombardment of Algiers in 1816 marked the end of the Barbary pirates' power in the Mediterranean. Slavery was gradually stamped out. Dutch warships patrolled Southeast Asia, and the British attacked the pirates of the South China Sea.

▶ In 1840 a British explorer named James Brooke became the rajah, or ruler, of Sarawak, on the island of Borneo. He organized a series of devastating attacks on the Dayak pirates.

53

# Piracy today

Piracy has never returned to the level of 300 years ago. But it has not completely disappeared, either. In the 1990s political groups have hijacked ships, threatening to kill crews and passengers if their demands are not met. Pirates in Southeast Asia have attacked local shipping as well as international supertankers and container ships. Luxury yachts in the Caribbean have also been attacked and robbed.

▶ Pirates still rely on speed and surprise. They use fast dinghies and arm themselves with deadly assault rifles. Large modern ships have only small crews, who can be easily overcome.

Modern pirates may just rob the crew of their watches, videos, cameras, and money. Or they may hijack the whole ship and try to sell its cargo.

People have always loved stories about pirates. In the 1700s, songs, plays, and novels were written about buccaneers. By the 1800s and early 1900s, storybook pirates were more famous than the real ones. People still laugh today at *The Pirates of Penzance*, a comic opera by Gilbert and Sullivan, first performed on April 3rd, 1880, at the Opera Comique in London. But remember the reality—there was nothing comic about the cold steel of a cutlass through the ribs or the sight of a blackjack's skull and crossbones.

► **Long John Silver, complete with wooden leg and parrot. He is the main character in the most famous pirate story of all, *Treasure Island*. It was written by the Scottish author Robert Louis Stevenson in 1881, for his stepson. It is about a map, some buried treasure, and a mutiny led by Long John Silver on board the *Hispaniola*.**

▲ **This scene of murder and mayhem comes from the 1995 movie *Cutthroat Island*. Ever since the 1920s, Hollywood has made movies that feature the adventures of** **romantic, swashbuckling buccaneers. Few of the movies have ever shown pirates as they really were—desperate, hungry, ragged, cruel, and violent fighting men.**

### Pirates in fiction

*The Coral Island* by R. M. Ballantyne. First published in 1857.

*Peter Pan* by J. M. Barrie. First published in 1904; first performed as a play in 1911.

*Treasure Island* by R. L. Stevenson. First published in 1883.

### Pirates in nonfiction

*Eyewitness Pirate* by Richard Platt. Published by Knopf in 1995.

*Life among the Pirates* by David Cordingly. Published by Random House in 1996.

*Pirate Fact and Fiction* by David Cordingly and John Falconer. Published by Collins & Brown Ltd. in 1992.

*Pirates and Treasure* by Saviour Pirotta. Published by Raintree Steck-Vaughn in 1995.

### Pirates in movies

*Cutthroat Island*, 1995, starring Geena Davis.

*Hook*, 1991, starring Robin Williams and Julia Roberts.

*Treasure Island—the Movie*, 1995, starring the Muppets.

There are many old movies, too. One of the best is *Captain Blood*, 1935, starring Errol Flynn and Olivia de Havilland.

# Rogues' gallery

### Alwilda
(active 400s A.D.)
This princess from Gotland, Sweden, is said to have turned pirate when her father tried to force her into marriage. She changed her mind about her husband-to-be when he captured her during a sea battle.

### Kanhoji Angria (died 1729)
Kanhoji Angria was the first of his family to lead attacks on British shipping off the west coast of India in the 1700s.

### Henry Avery ("Long Ben")
(1685–c. 1728)
Avery was the "Arch-Pirate," an Englishman who became famous for his brutal and highly profitable attack on the Mogul ship *Gang-i-Sawai* in the Arabian Sea.

### Aruj Barbarossa (died 1518) and Kheir-ed-din Barbarossa (died 1546)
The Greek-born Barbarossa (red beard) brothers founded the power of the Barbary corsairs in the 1500s, attacking Christian shipping and coastal towns around the Mediterranean.

### Jean Bart (1651–1702)
This fisherman's son from Dunkirk raided North Sea and English Channel fleets. He served in the Dutch navy and later became a successful privateer for the French. He made a famous escape in a small boat from Plymouth, England.

### Bartolomeo "el Portugués"
(active 1660s–1670s)
Famous for his lucky escapes, this Portuguese buccaneer was one of the first to be based in Jamaica. His luck finally ran out in a shipwreck.

### Sam "Black" Bellamy
(active 1715–1717)
English-born Sam Bellamy traveled to Cape Cod, Massachusetts, in about 1715. He went to Florida in search of Spanish treasure and turned pirate. He captured the *Whydah* in 1717 but died when it sank in a fierce storm.

### Stede Bonnet (died 1718)
Bonnet was a respectable middle-aged man who suddenly took up a life of crime. Blackbeard found his dress and manner hugely amusing. Bonnet was hanged at Charleston harbor in South Carolina in 1718.

### Anne Bonny (active 1719)
This Irishwoman left her husband for "Calico Jack" Rackham in the Bahamas. Women were banned from most pirate vessels in the 1700s, but she became one of the most famous fighters of her day. When Rackham was hanged in Jamaica, Bonny was pardoned because she was pregnant.

### Roche Brasiliano
(active 1670s)
This Dutch buccaneer lived in Brazil before turning up in Jamaica in the 1670s. A drunkard famous for his cruelty, he was elected pirate captain and he terrorized Spanish shipping.

### Nicholas Brown (died 1726)
Known as the "Grand Pirate," Brown was once given a royal pardon but went back to attacking shipping off Jamaica. He was captured by a childhood friend, John Drudge. When Brown died of his wounds, Drudge cut off his head and pickled it, in order to claim a reward.

### Madame Cheng
(active 1807–1810)
This ruthless woman took over her husband's pirate fleet when he died and turned it into a huge organization. She was famous throughout the South China Sea for her cruelty.

### Christopher Condent
(active 1718–1720)
This savage pirate came from Plymouth, England. In the Bahamas, he took to the Pirate Round and attacked merchant ships off Africa and Arabia. He settled in Madagascar and Mauritius before retiring to St. Malo in France.

### Cui Apu (died 1851)
This Chinese pirate commanded a fleet of over 500 junks in the South China Sea during the 1800s. His activities were put to an end by British warships.

### William Dampier
(1652–1715)
William Dampier came from England and fought alongside buccaneers in

Central America. Marooned on the Nicobar Islands in the Indian Ocean, he escaped in a canoe and wrote about his travels in *Voyage around the World* (1697). Dampier was a brilliant navigator and later explored the waters around Australia.

### Simon Danziger or Dansker (Dali Raïs or "Captain Devil") (died 1611)

This Dutch privateer sailed out of Marseilles in southern France in the 1600s, but took up service with the Barbary corsairs. He captured many Christian ships and taught the Muslims the seafaring skills required for the North Atlantic waters. He then changed sides again—only to be seized and hanged in Tunis.

### Howell Davis (active 1719)

A Welsh pirate, Davis attacked slaving ships off Africa's Guinea Coast. He was killed in an ambush at the Portuguese colony of Principe.

### Francis Drake (c. 1540–1596)

Drake was a great English seaman and explorer. In 1578–1580, he sailed around the world in the *Golden Hind*, engaged in piracy and privateering, and was knighted by Queen Elizabeth I on his return.

### Réné Duguay-Trouin (1673–1736)

This French corsair from St. Malo became so famous for his attacks on British shipping that he was made a French naval commander and was given many public honors.

### Peter Easton

(active 1607–1612)

Easton was an English pirate who commanded 17 ships and carried out attacks from Newfoundland to West Africa. Having won a fortune, he settled in the south of France and was made a marquis.

### Edward England (died c. 1720)

Edward England may in fact have been an Irishman named Jasper Seager. He sailed with Bartholomew Roberts on the Guinea Coast, but was later marooned in Mauritius.

### Eustace "the Black Monk"

(active 1200s)

This Flemish-born monk turned outlaw and raided shipping in the English Channel. He was said to have a pact with the devil and the power to make his ship invisible. But he was defeated in a sea battle in 1217 and had his head cut off.

### John Evans (active 1720s)

Captain John Evans was a Welsh sailor who ended up in Port Royal, Jamaica. In 1722 he and his shipmates raided the Jamaican coast from a *piragua* and captured many ships. Evans was shot in a quarrel with his bosun off Grand Cayman.

### Alexandre Exquemelin

(active 1660s–1690s)

Probably born in Normandy, France, Exquemelin was a surgeon who went to the Caribbean with the French West India Company and joined the Tortuga buccaneers. Back in Europe he wrote the famous *Bucaniers of America* (1678), and then returned to the Spanish Main in the 1690s.

### Jean Fleury or Florin

(died 1527)

One of the first French corsairs to attack a Spanish treasure fleet, Fleury was a privateer in the service of the Viscount of Dieppe.

### Antonio Fuët

(active 1660s–1690s)

This French pirate from Narbonne was known as "Captain Moidore." Once, when he was attacking a ship, Fuët ran out of shot and had to load up his cannon with *moidores*—these were a type of gold coin used in Portugal and Brazil.

### Klein Hänslein ("Little Jack") (died 1573)

This German pirate of the 1570s attacked shipping in the North Sea until he and his crew were captured and beheaded in Hamburg.

### Sir John Hawkins (1532–1595)

A privateer from Plymouth, in England, Hawkins was one of the first traders to ship slaves from West Africa to the Caribbean.

### Victor Hugues

(active 1790s)

Born in Marseilles, this Frenchman lost his business in Haiti when the slaves there demanded freedom. So he turned to piracy and made a fortune by raiding shipping out of Guadeloupe.

### Jan Jansz (Murad Raïs)

(active 1620s)

This Dutch privateer joined the Barbary corsairs and in 1627 led a Muslim fleet to Iceland, where they took slaves and plunder.

### John Paul Jones
(1747–1792)

Scottish-born Jones became an American hero in the War of Independence—he attacked ships in British waters, and was condemned as a traitor and pirate. Later a rear-admiral in the Russian navy, he died in France.

### William Kidd (c. 1645–1701)
Kidd was a Scottish sea captain who lived in New York City. He was commissioned as a privateer, but took up piracy in the Indian Ocean and was hanged in London in 1701.

### Lady Mary Killigrew
(active 1580s)
The Killigrews were secret backers of piracy in Cornwall. In 1583 a Spanish merchant ship was driven into the coast by storms. Lady Killigrew led a boarding party onto the vessel, killing the crew and stealing the cargo. She was sentenced to death for piracy but was let off.

### Jean Lafitte (active 1810s)
This French pirate attacked ships in the Caribbean and Indian Ocean. He became a big gangster in New Orleans, but was hailed as an all-American hero after defending the city against the British in 1812.

### François le Clerc
(active 1553–1554)
This French privateer was known as Jambe de Bois ("pegleg") because of his wooden leg. He attacked Spanish ships off Puerto Rico and Hispaniola, and sacked the port of Santiago de Cuba with eight ships and 300 men.

### François l'Ollonois (Jean-David Nau) (active 1660s)
Born in Sables d'Olonne, France, Nau became one of the cruelest of all the buccaneers. He took part in many horrible attacks on the Spanish Main but was himself captured by Indians, hacked to bits, and burned over a fire.

### George Lowther (active 1720s)
Lowther sailed to West Africa as second mate on a merchant ship called the *Gambia Castle*, joined up with some soldiers on board and seized the vessel, changing its name to the *Delivery*. He took up piracy along the coasts of the Caribbean and North America. In 1728 his pirates were careening their ship when they came under attack. Lowther is thought to have shot himself, and some of his crew were arrested and hanged.

### Henry Mainwaring
(1587–1653)
This English knight was a pirate hunter who ended up turning to piracy himself. He was based in Morocco from 1612, and spent four years attacking merchant shipping in the Mediterranean. Then he returned to England and received a pardon.

### William Marsh or de Marisco (died 1242)
A violent enemy of King Henry III of England, Marsh based himself on Lundy Island in the Bristol Channel. From there he raided ships in the Irish Sea and demanded ransoms for his captives.

### Henry Morgan (c. 1635–1688)
This Welsh buccaneer was kidnapped as a youth at the port of Bristol, England, and shipped to Barbados. In the Caribbean he became the most famous organizer of buccaneer armies against the Spanish, carrying out raids with military precision, but without mercy. He was honored by the British authorities in Jamaica before dying of drink.

### Grace O' Malley
(active 1560s–1580s)
This Irish noblewoman led attacks on shipping off the west coast of Ireland. In 1593 she won a pardon and a pension from Elizabeth I. She handed over to her sons.

### James Plantain (active 1720s)
Born in Jamaica, this pirate set up his base on Madagascar. He built a fortress at Ranter Bay and declared himelf "king." He kept many wives and was said to live in luxury.

### John Rackham ("Calico Jack") (died 1720)
John Rackham and Anne Bonny set up in partnership in the Bahamas in 1719. Rackham was hanged in Jamaica in 1720. "If he had fought like a man," said Anne, "he need not have been hanged like a dog."

### Raga (active 1820s)
Chief of the Malay pirates in the Straits of Makassar, Raga took many European ships and beheaded their crews. His base at Kuala Batu, Sumatra, was destroyed by an American task force.

### Rahmah bin Jabr
(c. 1756–1826)
The most famous pirate of the Persian Gulf, this one-eyed captain plundered shipping for 50 years. At the age of 70, in battle with the whole fleet of Bahrain, he set fire to the gunpowder magazine on his own dhow, blowing half the enemy (and himself) sky high.

### Sir Walter Raleigh
(1552–1618)
An Elizabethan courtier and navigator, Raleigh fitted out many privateering expeditions in order to fund a new colony in Virginia. On the death of Queen Elizabeth I, Raleigh's fortunes changed. In 1616 he persuaded James I to send him on another search for gold, but he returned empty-handed and was beheaded.

### Mary Read (active 1719–1721)
This Englishwoman, who often dressed as a man, fought as a soldier in Flanders and owned a tavern before sailing to the Caribbean. When her ship was captured by Rackham and Bonny, she joined their crew. Like Bonny, Read escaped the gallows because she was expecting a baby. She died of fever in Jamaica in 1721.

### Basil Ringrose (c. 1653–1686)
This English surgeon traveled through Panama with Bartholomew Sharp and his buccaneers in 1680–1682, and wrote about his travels. He was killed in Mexico.

### Bartholomew Roberts ("Black Bart") (1682–1722)
A Welsh pirate captain, Roberts is said to have seized 400 ships off West Africa and in the Caribbean. His biggest coup was capturing the *Sagrada Familia*, a Portuguese vessel carrying a fortune in coins, diamonds, and goods from Brazil.

### Abraham Samuel
(active 1690s)
Of mixed African and European descent, Jamaican Abraham Samuel proclaimed himself pirate "king" of Port Dauphin, on Madagascar, in the days of the Pirate Round.

### Richard Sawkins (died 1680)
Buccaneer captain in the Caribbean, Sawkins attacked Spanish shipping and outwitted the British navy. He fought in Panama and was killed there at Pueblo Nuevo.

### Störtebeker (active 1390s)
This former merchant formed a pirate band called "The Friends of God and Enemies of the World." They sailed the Baltic Sea and attacked the city of Bergen, in Norway. He was executed in 1402.

### Robert Surcouf (1773–1827)
Originally from the corsair haven of St. Malo, this famous French privateer attacked British ships in the Indian Ocean with devastating success. He captured the *Triton* in 1795 and the *Kent* in 1800.

### Sweyn Forkbeard (died 1014)
Viking king of Denmark, Sweyn defeated and killed his own father, Harald Bluetooth. He led many piratical raids against England, receiving huge sums of money in payment of ransom demands.

### Edward Teach or Thatch (Blackbeard) (died 1718)
A brutal pirate with his beard and long hair tied in braids, Blackbeard terrorized the North American coast before being killed in battle. His fame soon spread around the world.

### Thomas Tew (died 1695)
Born in Rhode Island, Tew commanded a ship called the *Amity* and attacked Mogul shipping in the Indian Ocean. He made a fortune from his first voyage but was killed on his second.

### Charles Vane (died 1720)
When Vane came to New Providence in 1718, he was already known as a boastful, bullying desperado. He terrorized Caribbean shipping but lost his ship in a storm in 1720. He was brought to trial in Spanish Town, Jamaica, and was hanged.

### Francis Verney (1584–1615)
This English gentleman "turned Turk" and went off to become a Barbary corsair at the age of 23. Based in Algiers, Sir Francis attacked English shipping but was captured by a Christian galley and enslaved.

### John Ward (Yusuf Raïs)
(c. 1553–1622)
An English sea captain turned Barbary corsair, Ward was based in Tunis, where he died of plague.

# Glossary

*To find out the names for parts of a ship and sails, turn to pages 34–37.*

**archaeologist** Someone who studies historical remains, such as ruins and shipwrecks.

**backstaff** An instrument once used to measure a ship's position.

**ballast** Any heavy material used to weigh down a ship to make it stable.

**barnacles** Small creatures that encrust underwater rocks and ships' timbers.

**bilge water** Foul water that collected in the bottom of old sailing ships.

**blackjack** Any of the black-and-white pirate flags used from the 1690s onward.

**blackjack**

**block and tackle** Pulley and ropes.

**blockade** To prevent shipping or supplies reaching a port.

**booty** Goods that are stolen or won by violence.

**bosun** (or boatswain) The foreman of a crew.

**bowsprit** A long spar sticking out from the bow at the front of a sailing ship.

**buccaneer** One of the outlaws who settled on Caribbean islands from the 1630s onward and took up piracy.

**cannibalism** Eating other people.

**cannon** A large gun mounted on wheels.

**capstan** A winding machine pushed around by the crew of a sailing vessel to raise the anchor.

**caravel** A small three-masted sailing ship used by the Spanish and Portuguese in the 1400s and early 1500s.

**careen** To beach a ship for cleaning and repairs.

**castle** A high fighting deck on either end of a medieval warship. The term "forecastle" (front deck) survived as fo'c'sle.

**caulk** To make a wooden ship waterproof with oakum and tar.

**chart** A map of oceans and coastlines.

**colony** (1) An overseas settlement. (2) A country ruled by another.

**commission** Authorization for a privateer to attack enemy shipping.

**compass** A magnetic navigational instrument used to find north.

**compensation** Money paid to make up for an injury or loss.

**corsair** (1) A pirate or privateer, especially from the Mediterranean Sea or northern France. (2) The ship used by a corsair.

**cutlass** A type of naval sword said to have been developed from the hunting knives of the first buccaneers.

**dhow** An Arab sailing ship with triangular sails.

**doubloon** A Spanish gold coin.

**dugout** A canoe hollowed out from a tree trunk.

**empire** A large group of territories ruled by a single government.

**evidence** Facts put before a court of law during a trial.

**capstan**

**figurehead** A carved and painted wooden figure placed at the front of a ship.

**figurehead**

**filibuster** (or *flibustier*) A French buccaneer in the Caribbean.

**first mate** The second-in-command of a merchant or pirate ship.

**fore and aft** At the front and at the back of a ship.

**fort** A building raised for defense, protected by guns.

**freebooter** Any pirate, privateer, or raider.

**galleon** A large sailing ship used by the Spanish in the 1500s and 1600s.

**galley** (1) Any warship that was powered by oar and sail. (2) The kitchen on a ship.

**gibbet**

**gibbet** Public gallows or posts used for displaying executed criminals to the public.

**"go on the account"** To become a pirate.

**grappling iron** Metal hooks used to gain hold of an enemy ship and board it.

**grenade** A small bomb thrown by hand.

**grappling iron**

**hardtack** Stale ship's biscuit.

**haven** A safe harbor or anchorage.

**hijack** To seize a ship or its cargo.

**hoard** A pile of hidden treasure.

**hull** The outer shell of a ship.

**Jolly Roger** Any pirate flag.

**junk** A large wooden sailing ship used by the Chinese.

**keel** A single timber running along the bottom of a ship's hull.

**knot** (1) A method of tying one or more ropes. (2) Speed—one nautical mile per hour (1.15 mph).

**lee** The sheltered side of a ship or shore —the opposite of "windward" or "weather," the exposed side.

**letters of marque** Official papers of authorization, issued to privateers.

**logbook** The daily record of a ship's voyage.

**long ship** A sailing ship used by Viking sea raiders.

**magazine** A gunpowder store.

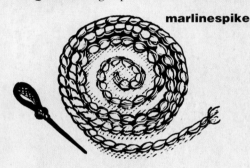

**marlinespike**

**marlinespike** A pointed metal tool used for working on ropes.

**maroon** To leave someone behind on a desert island, as punishment.

**merchant ship** A trading ship carrying goods.

**musket** A long-barreled hand gun, an early version of the rifle.

**musket**

**New World** A European term for the newly discovered Americas.

**oakum** Rope fibers used in caulking.

**pieces-of-eight**

**pieces-of-eight** Type of Spanish coinage.

*piragua* A war canoe used by the buccaneers in the Caribbean.

**pirate** Someone who attacks shipping or coastal settlements illegally.

**Pirate Round** A pirate voyage from North America or the Caribbean to West Africa and the Indian Ocean, and back again.

**plantation** A large estate producing crops such as tobacco, sugarcane, or cotton.

**plunder** Items that have been stolen or seized by force.

**powder horn** A container used to hold the gunpowder for a musket.

**powder horn**

*prahu* A light, fast boat used by the Dayak pirates of Southeast Asia.

**privateer** (1) A person given legal authority to raid enemy merchant shipping and to share in the booty. (2) The ship used by a privateer.

**prize** An enemy ship captured in battle.

*raïs* A sea captain in the service of the Barbary corsairs.

**ram** The long pointed front of an ancient galley, used for sinking the enemy.

**ransom** A fee demanded for the release of a captive.

**Redemptionist** One of the Christian priests who raised funds to buy back Christian slaves from the Barbary Coast.

**rig** The masts and sails of a ship.

**rigging** The system of ropes used to support the masts and sails of a ship.

**rover** A seafarer, often a pirate or rogue.

**rudder** A hinged board at the back of a ship, for steering.

**rum** A strong alcoholic drink made from sugarcane.

**sailcloth** Tough canvas used for sails.

**schooner** A fast two-masted sailing ship.

**scurvy** A disease of the skin and gums caused by lack of vitamin C. Sailors often suffered from it because they did not eat enough fruit and vegetables.

**scuttle** To sink a ship in one's possession on purpose.

**seam** The gap between two planks on a wooden ship.

**slave** Someone deprived of their freedom in order to work for someone else.

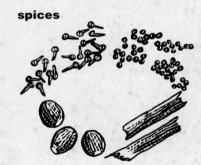

**sloop** A swift single-masted sailing vessel.

**smuggler** Someone who imports goods illegally, to avoid paying tax on them.

**Spanish Main** (1) Those parts of the American mainland conquered by the Spanish. (2) The whole Caribbean.

**spar** Any wooden pole used for supporting sails.

**Spice Islands** An old-fashioned name for the islands of Southeast Asia where spices are grown.

**spices**

**splice** To join together two ropes.

**tavern** An inn or a bar.

**tax** Money paid to the government.

**treasure** Goods of great value, such as gold and silver.

**trireme** A galley with three banks of oars, used by the Greeks and Romans.

**"turn Turk"** (1) Of Christian sailors, to become a Barbary corsair. (2) To change sides.

**typhoon** A violent storm in the Pacific Ocean.

**Viking** A Scandinavian sea raider of about 1,000 years ago.

**watch** Being on the lookout, or keeping guard.

**yard** The crossbar supporting a sail.

# Index

## A

*Adventure Galley* 34-35, 36
Africa 16, 22-26
Alwilda 56
*Amity* 31
anchor 35
Angria family 28
Angria, Kanhoji 29, 56
Anstis, Thomas 50
Arabs 23
archaeology 6, 7, 60
Avery, Henry 30, 31, 40, 50, 56

## B

backstaff 41, 60
Baltic Sea 12
Barbarossa brothers 25, 56
Barbary Coast 23, 24-25
Bart, Jean 13, 56
Bartolomeo "el Portugués" 17, 56
Bellamy, Sam 6, 7, 56
bilge water 43, 60
Blackbeard *see* Teach, Edward
blackjacks 40, 60
Bonnet, Stede 21, 56
Bonny, Anne 19, 56
Borneo 33, 53
boucan 16
bowsprit 34, 35, 60
Brasiliano, Roche 17, 56
Brethren of the Coast 16
Britain 10, 18, 21, 28, 53
Brittany 12, 13
Brooke, James 53
Brown, Nicholas 56
buccaneer 5, 7, 16-17, 18, 19, 35, 46, 60

## C

"Calico Jack" *see* Rackham, John
cannibalism 43, 60
cannon 34, 37, 46-47, 60
capstan 34, 35, 60
caravel 14, 15, 60

careening 27, 60
Caribbean 5, 14, 16-17, 20, 35, 46, 49, 54
Cartagena 5
caulking 27, 60
chart 41, 60
Cheng I 33
Chinese 32, 33, 40, 43, 46, 53
Christians 24, 25, 31, 39
Cilicians 8-9, 39, 48
Clifford, Barry 7
Columbus, Christopher 15
compass 41, 60
compensation 45, 60
Condent, Christopher 40, 56
corsair 5, 13, 15, 23, 24, 25, 60
Cuba 14, 16
Cui Apu 32, 56
cutlass 19, 46, 47, 60

## D

Dampier, William 7, 56
Danziger, Simon 25, 57
Davis, Howell 23, 41, 57
Davy Jones's locker 49
Dayaks 33, 53
Defoe, Daniel 27
*Derby* 28
dhow 39, 60
doubloon 49, 60
Drake, Sir Francis 5, 15, 57
dugout 17, 60
Duguay-Trouin, Réné 13, 57

## E

East Indiaman 28, 29, 38, 48
Easton, Peter 57
England, Edward 26, 57
English Channel 12, 13
Eustace "the Black Monk" 12, 57
Evans, John 57
execution 50-51
Exquemelin, Alexandre 7, 57

## F

*Fancy* 30

*Fateh Muhammad* 50
filibuster 5, 60
films 55
flags 40-41
Fleury, Jean 14, 57
France 9, 10, 16
freebooter 5, 60
Fuët, Antonio 57

## G

galleon 14, 35, 38, 39, 60
galley 8, 38, 39, 60
*Gang-i-Sawai* 30
gibbet 50, 60
Gilbert and Sullivan 55
grappling iron 37, 60
Greeks 4, 9, 55
Greenland 10
Guinea Coast 23, 26, 31
gunpowder 34, 46, 47

## H

Hands, Israel 46
Hänslein, Klein 12, 57
hardtack 43, 60
Hawkins, Sir John 57
hijacking 54, 60
Hispaniola 16, 55
Hugues, Victor 57

## I

Iceland 10, 25
Ilanun pirates 33
India 30
Indian Ocean 23, 26, 29, 31, 32
Ireland 10, 12

## J

Jamaica 16, 18, 19
Jansz, Jan 25, 57
Japan 33
Jolly Roger 40, 60
Jones, John Paul 58
junk 38, 60

## K

Kidd, William 31, 34-35, 44, 50, 58
Killigrew, Lady Mary 58
knots 37, 61

# Acknowledgments

The publishers would like to thank the following
illustrators for their contributions to this book:

**John Batchelor** pages 34-35, 36;
**Richard Berridge** (Specs Art) 29*br*, 33*bl* & *br*, 50-51, 53*cr*;
**Peter Dennis** (Linda Rogers Associates)
4-5, 6-7, 14-15, 16*b*, 17*b*, 18*l*, 20-21;
**Richard Draper** 7*br*, 24*cl*, 27*br*, 40*t*, 41*tr*, 43*br*, 46-47*t*,
48*tr*, 49*cr*;
**Francesca D'Ottavi** 42-43, 44, 45*t*, 46-47*b*, 48-49;
**Christian Hook** 8-9, 10-11, 12*tr*, 13*br*, 41*b*, 55;
**John Lawrence** (Virgil Pomfret) 9*br*, 10*cl*, 13*tl*, 17*tr*, 23*bl*,
26*tr*, 29*tr*, 31*cr*, 32*tr*, 37*b*, 60-61;
**Angus McBride** (Linden Artists) 22-23, 24*tr*, 25*br*, 26-27;
**Clare Melinsky** 56-59;
**Nicki Palin** 19*b*, 28-29, 30-31, 31*tr*, 32*b*, 33*cl*;
**Shirley Tourret** (B. L. Kearley Ltd) 12*bl*, 16*tr*, 17*tl*, 18*r*,
19*tr*, 20*tl* & *br*, 25*tl*, 26*bl*, 30*tr*, 33*tr*, 37*tl* & *tr*, 45*bl*, 50*bl*;
**Thomas Trojer** 38-39;
**Richard Willis** (Linden Artists) 52-53.

Page symbols and border rope by **John Lawrence**.

The publishers would also like to thank the following
for supplying photographs for this book:

13 **The Masters and Fellows of
Corpus Christi College, Cambridge**
49, 54*b* **Mary Evans Picture Library**
54*t* **The Kobal Collection**
5, 7, 15, 24, 40, 53 **National Maritime Museum**
51 **Peter Newark's Historical Pictures**
43 & 44 **Public Record Office**